D0571914

Shelley

Lyrical Romantic

First published in Great Britain by Brockhampton Press,
a member of the Hodder Headline Group,
20 Bloomsbury Street, London WC1B 3QA

ISBN 1 86019 397 8

Created and produced by Flame Tree Publishing,
part of The Foundry Creative Media Company Limited,
The Long House, Antrobus Road, Chiswick, London W4 5HY

Special thanks to
Kate Brown and Kelley Doak for their work on this series

Printed and bound in U.A.E.

Shelley

Lyrical Romantic

Written and Compiled by
K. E. SULLIVAN

Contents

Introduction

A poet is a nightingale who sits in darkness and sings to cheer its
own solitude with sweet sounds.
Percy Bysshe Shelley

Percy Bysshe Shelley was probably the most unconventional yet quintessentially romantic poet of his age, an intense and idealistic man of immeasurable imagination and energy. He was just twenty-nine when he died, but his passionate spirit eclipsed his contemporaries and he has come to be considered one of the most radical and gifted poets of the English language. He was both admired and hated by the critics, and indeed by his inner circle of acquaintances, unanimously inspiring passionate feelings in all who knew him. Southey said of him, 'With all his genius (and I think most highly of it), he was a base, bad man.' Carlyle noted, 'Weak in Genius, weak in character (for these two always go together); a poor, thin, spasmodic, hectic, shrill and pallid being ...'

But this hectic, effeminate and pale being fired his closest friends with enthusiasm, and filled his devotees with awe. Byron, who both admired and championed Shelley, said to a detractor, 'You were all brutally mistaken about Shelley, who was, without exception, the *best* and least selfish man I ever knew ...' He was an extravagant romantic, an intellectual melodramatic, a highly strung and ethereal man.

Shelley was born in Warnham, Sussex on 4 August 1792 to a wealthy, pretentious family. His father was a solicitor and a Member of Parliament, a man of gross ostentations and assumed enlightenment. His mother was a local beauty, accustomed to English country living and quite dismayed by her foppish young son. He had several sisters and he became used to being the centre of attention in a household of

women; his later domestic arrangements reflected this. When Shelley was ten he was sent to Syon House Academy, and two years later he entered Eton preparatory school.

Eton left a bitter mark on Shelley, for he shunned the traditions to the despair of his seniors and colleagues. He became the object of 'Shelley Hunts' and he was called 'mad Shelley'. He strove to live up to his name, feigning sightings and evocations of the devil and writing his first novel before he left for Oxford at the age of eighteen. He was a delicate youth, but what he lacked in stature he made up for in sagacity, in imaginative power, in ardour and in fortitude. He excelled in the classics, revelled in learning. In his first year at University College, Oxford, where he arrived in 1810, he published his first book of verse, entitled *Original Poetry by Victor and Cazire*, co-authored by his sister Elizabeth.

At Oxford Shelley befriended Thomas Jefferson Hogg, who shared his radical spirit. After five months both were expelled for the publication of a pamphlet entitled *The Necessity of Atheism*, an act which shocked his family and led to his estrangement and virtual disinheritance. Shelley moved to London in straitened circumstances, where he fell in love with a sixteen-year-old innkeeper's daughter called Harriet Westbrook, with whom he eloped and later married in Scotland. They had a nomadic and unstable existence, travelling across the British Isles in an attempt to realize Shelley's dream of founding a utopian community of like-minded individuals. They travelled to Dublin, where they distributed pamphlets in an attempt to excite an Irish revolt, and then they returned to England and settled in the Lake District, where Shelley had notions of meeting and communing with the great Lake poets, Wordsworth, Coleridge and Southey. Their first daughter, Ianthe, was born in 1813, the same year that he made Southey's acquaintance and struck up a friendship with the philosopher William Godwin. Shelley had read Godwin's book, *An Enquiry Concerning Political Justice*, at school and he had been profoundly moved by its message. The inspiration of that work and its author were expressed in his poem 'Queen Mab', published in 1813.

Shelley remarried Harriet in a religious ceremony three years after their initial marriage in order to assure his children of their legitimacy, but they separated two months later. It was at this time that Shelley met Godwin's daughter, Mary Wollstonecraft Godwin, and they eloped together, along with Mary's half-sister, Claire Claremont, to the Continent. Mary and Shelley were well suited both in temperament and in intellectual prowess, and Harriet, who was left pregnant in England, was all but forgotten until her suicide two years later. Claire, Mary and Shelley travelled to Europe, History of a Six Weeks Tour produced on the way, and their son William (Willmouse to Shelley) was born a year later. Shelley's grandfather had died, leaving him some money, and their financial situation was eased slightly.

Although he still considered himself a reformer (he wanted to free 'mankind, to purify life of its misery and evil') he was largely impractical. Indeed, the critic Matthew Arnold called him 'a beautiful, ineffectual angel, beating in the void his luminous wings in vain'. He concentrated increasingly on his poetry and in 1816 met Byron on Lake Geneva, where Claire became pregnant with Byron's child and Mary embarked on her novel Frankenstein. Shelley had begun to receive some critical encouragement for his work, in particular for his poem Alastor, and he found renewed energy for his craft. They returned to England where Shelley continued his political work and began his great revolutionary masterpiece, eventually published as The Revolt of Islam, in 1818.

His children by Harriet were taken away from him, and numbed by his situation and disheartened by the political situation in England, the trio left once again for Italy, where he wrote works which represent his greatest achievement as a poet.

The living arrangements were largely undisclosed, but it

was suggested that Shelley and his two women did share a close relationship which escaped the bounds of being purely platonic. Claire was deeply in love with Byron who refused to see her, but with whom she shared their daughter Allegra, and there is some evidence that she may have borne Shelley's child as well, although all traces of this were swept away and the child fostered out. His daughter Clara and his son Willmouse died and Mary suffered depressions, which were deepened by her impatient fury and jealousy of Claire. Their third child Percy was born in 1819, but Mary never really recovered her bantering nature and could not longer play the intellectual foil to her husband.

But this period of unhappiness nurtured Shelley's poetic spirit. He wrote *Prometheus Unbound*, *The Mask of Anarchy*, 'Ode to the West Wind', *Peter Bell the Third* and *The Cenci*, which was Shelley's only contribution to the theatre. 'Ode to the West Wind' was called by Stephen Spender, 'the most symphonic poem in the English language' and the beauty and musicality of his lyrical work is still unsurpassed today. He had a gift for lyricism, a pure and true eloquence which celebrates the sensual, the aural. He went on to write *A Defence of Poetry*, and upon the death of Keats in 1819, *Adonaïs*, a tribute to his close friend. *Adonaïs* is considered to be the most elegant and perfect of his works, with exquisitely apt translations from Latin, Greek, Italian and Spanish. Mary wrote, 'There is much in *Adonaïs* which seems to be more applicable to Shelley himself than to the young and gifted poet whom he mourned.'

Shelley's work is one of contrasting styles and themes. He was as adept at the poetry of nature as Wordsworth; his evocation of the senses matched Keats; his Gothic horrors were more sophisticated than even his wife's. He latched on to a cause and drained it; he was inspired by everything he saw. Nothing was too insignificant as a subject for his work. He wrote of love, politics, the tyranny of the spirit; he wrote of beauty, the ephemeral; he wrote of nature.

Shelley continued to write prolifically as they travelled. They were joined by Byron, and then Leigh Hunt at Pisa in Italy and Shelley felt at last that he was beginning to draw together the strings of a community of like-minded individuals. But instead of being inspired by the interchange of ideas and poetic fashions, Shelley found Byron a stifling presence, and in 1822 he moved with his two women to the seaside at Lerici. Shortly thereafter Allegra died, and Mary suffered a serious miscarriage.

Shelley had had a series of affairs outside his *menage à trois*, including one with Emilia Viviani, for whom he wrote 'Epipsychidion', and Jane Williams, for whom he wrote a number of lyrics, but Mary had never ceased to adore him. He loved her deeply, and her miscarriage and subsequent ill-health filled him with despair. But, once again, suffering caused his spirit to soar and he wrote the elegant and intellectual lyric poems which were to crown his career.

In the summer of 1822, Shelley travelled with Edward Williams, the husband of Jane, and a cabin boy across the Gulf of Spezia to visit Byron. They never returned. A storm overturned their boat and their bodies were missing for ten days. Shelley's was found near Viareggio on 18 July, a volume of Aeschylus soaked in a pocket. A month later, Byron, Hunt and Edward Trelawney burned Shelley's body on the beach at Viareggio, and placed his ashes at the Protestant Cemetery in Rome, next to the body of his beloved Keats. A few days before he died, he said, 'If I die tomorrow, I shall have lived to be older than my grandfather; I am ninety years old.'

Author's Note

Shelley's poetry has a lightness of touch and a musicality unequalled either before or since his time. The works which follow have been chosen to represent the wide diversity of his skill.

Chronology

1792   Percy Bysshe Shelley born 4 August at Warnham, Sussex.

1802   Attends Syon House Academy in Isleworth.

1804   Attends Eton.

1810   *Zastrozzi* published.
        Attends University College, Oxford.
        Meets Thomas Jefferson Hogg.

1811   Publishes *The Necessity of Atheism* with Hogg.
        Expelled from Oxford.
        Elopes with Harriet Westbrook.
        Meets Southey.

1812   Begins 'Queen Mab'.

1813   Daughter Ianthe born.

1814   Marries Harriet in a church ceremony. Harriet leaves him two months later. Elopes to Europe with Mary Godwin and Jane (Claire) Clairemont.
        Son Charles Bysshe born to Harriet.

1815	Writes 'Alastor' and 'Essay on Christianity'.
1816	Son William born to Mary. Travels to Geneva with William, Mary and Claire. Meets Byron there.
	Writes 'Mont Blanc' and 'Hymn to Intellectual Beauty'.
	Harriet commits suicide. Marries Mary.
1817	Loses custody of his children with Harriet. Writes *The Revolt of Islam* and 'Prince Athanase'.
	Daughter Clara born to Mary.
1818	Travels to Italy. Writes 'Rosalind and Helen', 'Lines Written among the Euganean Hills', 'Julian and Maddalo' and begins *Prometheus Unbound*. Clara dies.
1819	William dies. Writes *The Cenci*, 'Mask of Anarchy', 'Cyclops' and *Peter Bell the Third*. Son Percy Florence born to Mary.
1821	Writes *Epipsychidion*, *A Defence of Poetry* and 'Adonaïs'.
1822	Meets Trelawney. Writes *Charles I*. Drowned near La Spezia in Italy on 8 July. Body found 18 July. Mock funeral and body burned on the beach by Byron, Hunt and Trelawney. Ashes buried in the Protestant Cemetery in Rome.

Queen Mab
──── EXTRACT ────

I

HOW WONDERFUL is Death,
Death and his brother Sleep!
One, pale as yonder waning moon,
With lips of lurid blue;
The other, rosy as the morn
When throned on ocean's wave,
It blushes o'er the world:
Yet both so passing wonderful!

Hath then the gloomy Power
Whose reign is in the tainted sepulchres
Seized on her sinless soul
Must then that peerless form
Which love and admiration cannot view
Without a beating heart, those azure veins
Which steal like streams along a field of snow
That lovely outline, which is fair
As breathing marble, perish?
Must putrefaction's breath
Leave nothing of this heavenly sight
But loathsomeness and ruin?
Spare nothing but a gloomy theme,
On which the lightest heart might moralise?
Or is it only a sweet slumber
Stealing o'er sensation,
Which the breath of roseate morning
Chaseth into darkness?
Will Ianthe wake again,
And give that faithful bosom joy
Whose sleepless spirit waits to catch
Light, life, and rapture, from her smile?

Yes! she will wake again,
Although her glowing limbs are motionless,
And silent those sweet lips,
Once breathing eloquence
That might have soothed a tiger's rage,
Or thawed the cold heart of a conqueror.
Her dewy eyes are closed,
And on their lids, whose texture fine
Scarce hides the dark blue orbs beneath,
The baby Sleep is pillowed:
Her golden tresses shade
The bosom's stainless pride,
Curling like tendrils of the parasite
Around a marble column.

Hark! whence that rushing sound?
'Tis like the wondrous strain
That round a lonely ruin swells,
Which, wandering on the echoing shore,
The enthusiast hears at evening:
'Tis softer than the west wind's sigh;
'Tis wilder than the unmeasured notes
Of that strange lyre whose strings
The genii of the breezes sweep:
Those lines of rainbow light
Are like the moonbeams when they fall
Through some cathedral window, but the teints
Are such as may not find
Comparison on earth.

Behold the chariot of the Fairy Queen!
Celestial coursers paw the unyielding air;
Their filmy pennons at her word they furl,
And stop obedient to the reins of light:
These the Queen of Spells drew in,

She spread a charm around the spot,
And leaning graceful from the ethereal car,
Long did she gaze, and silently,
Upon the slumbering maid.

Oh! not the visioned poet in his dreams,
When silvery clouds float through the wildered brain,
When every sight of lovely, wild, and grand,
Astonishes, enraptures elevates
When fancy at a glance combines
The wondrous and the beautiful,
So bright, so fair, so wild a shape
Hath ever yet beheld,
As that which reined the coursers of the air,
And poured the magic of her gaze
Upon the sleeping maid.

The broad and yellow moon
Shone dimly through her form
That form of faultless symmetry;
The pearly and pellucid car
Moved not the moonlight's line;
'Twas not an earthly pageant;
Those who had looked upon the sight,
Passing all human glory,
Saw not the yellow moon,
Saw not the mortal scene,
Heard not the night-wind's rush,
Heard not an earthly sound,
Saw but the fairy pageant,
Heard but the heavenly strains
That filled the lonely dwelling.

The Fairy's frame was slight; yon fibrous cloud,
That catches but the palest tinge of even,
And which the straining eye can hardly seize
When melting into eastern twilight's shadow,
Were scarce so thin, so slight; but the fair star,
That gems the glittering coronet of morn,
Sheds not a light so mild, so powerful,
As that which, bursting from the Fairy's form,
Spread a purpureal halo round the scene,
Yet with an undulating motion,
Swayed to her outline gracefully.
From her celestial car
The Fairy Queen descended,
And thrice she waved her wand
Circled with wreaths of amaranth:
Her thin and misty form
Moved with the moving air,
And the clear silver tones,
As thus she spoke, were such
As are unheard by all but gifted ear.

Fairy. Stars! your balmiest influence shed!
Elements! your wrath suspend!
Sleep, Ocean, in the rocky bounds
That circle thy domain!
Let not a breath be seen to stir
Around yon grass-grown ruin's height,
Let even the restless gossamer
Sleep on the moveless air!
Soul of Ianthe! thou,
Judged alone worthy of the envied boon
That waits the good and the sincere; that waits
Those who have struggled, and with resolute will
Vanquished earth's pride and meanness, burst the chains,
The icy chains of custom, and have shone

The day-stars of their age; – Soul of Ianthe!
Awake! arise!

Sudden arose
Ianthe's Soul; it stood
All beautiful in naked purity,
The perfect semblance of its bodily frame.
Instinct with inexpressible beauty and grace,
Each stain of earthliness
Had passed away, it reassumed
Its native dignity, and stood
Immortal amid ruin.
Upon the couch the body lay,
Wrapt in the depth of slumber:
Its features were fixed and meaningless,
Yet animal life was there,
And every organ yet performed
Its natural functions; 'twas a sight
Of wonder to behold the body and soul.
The self-same lineaments, the same
Marks of identity were there;
Yet, oh how different! One aspires to heaven,
Pants for its sempiternal heritage,
And ever-changing, ever-rising still,
Wantons in endless being.
The other, for a time the unwilling sport
Of circumstance and passion, struggles on;
Fleets through its sad duration rapidly;
Then like a useless and worn-out machine,
Rots, perishes and passes.

Fairy. Spirit! who hast dived so deep;
Spirit! who hast soared so high;
Thou the fearless, thou the mild,
Accept the boon thy worth hath earned,
Ascend the car with me.

Spirit. Do I dream? Is this new feeling
But a visioned ghost of slumber?
If indeed I am a soul,
A free, a disembodied soul,
Speak again to me.

Fairy. I am the Fairy MAB: to me 'tis given
The wonders of the human world to keep.
The secrets of the immeasurable past,
In the unfailing consciences of men,
Those stern, unflattering chroniclers, I find:
The future, from the causes which arise
In each event, I gather: not the sting
Which retributive memory implants
In the hard bosom of the selfish man;
Nor that ecstatic and exulting throb
Which virtue's votary feels when he sums up
The thoughts and actions of a well-spent day,
Are unforeseen, unregistered by me:
And it is yet permitted me, to rend
The veil of mortal frailty, that the spirit,
Clothed in its changeless purity, may know
How soonest to accomplish the great end
For which it hath its being, and may taste
That peace, which, in the end, all life will share.
This is the meed of virtue; happy Soul,
Ascend the car with me!

The chains of earth's immurement
Fell from Ianthe's spirit;
They shrank and brake like bandages of straw
Beneath a wakened giant's strength.
She knew her glorious change,
And felt in apprehension uncontrolled
New raptures opening round:
Each day-dream of her mortal life,
Each frenzied vision of the slumbers
That closed each well-spent day
Seemed now to meet reality.

The Fairy and the Soul proceeded;
The silver clouds disparted;
And as the car of magic they ascended,
Again the speechless music swelled,
Again the coursers of the air
Unfurled their azure pennons, and the Queen,
Shaking the beamy reins,
Bade them pursue their way.

The magic car moved on.
The night was fair, and countless stars
Studded heaven's dark blue vault,
Just o'er the eastern wave
Peeped the first faint smile of morn:
The magic car moved on
From the celestial hoofs
The atmosphere in flaming sparkles flew,
And where the burning wheels
Eddied above the moutain's loftiest peak,
Was traced a line of lightning.
Now it flew far above a rock,
The utmost verge of earth,
The rival of the Andes, whose dark brow

Lowered o'er the silver sea.
Far, far below the chariot's path,
Calm as a slumbering babe,
Tremendous Ocean lay.
The mirror of its stillness showed
The pale and waning stars,
The chariot's fiery track,
And the grey light of morn
Tinging those fleecy clouds
That canopied the dawn.
Seemed it, that the chariot's way
Lay through the midst of an immense concave,
Radiant with million constellations, tinged
With shades of infinite colour,
And semicircled with a belt
Flashing incessant meteors.

The magic car moved on.
As they approached their goal,
The coursers seemed to gather speed;
The sea no longer was distinguished; earth
Appeared a vast and shadowy sphere;
The sun's unclouded orb
Rolled through the black concave;
Its rays of rapid light
Parted around the chariot's swifter course,
And fell, like Ocean's feathery spray
Dashed from the boiling surge
Before a vessel's prow.

The magic car moved on.
Earth's distant orb appeared
The smallest light that twinkles in the heaven;
Whilst round the chariot's way
Innumerable systems rolled,

And countless spheres diffused
An ever varying glory.
It was a sight of wonder: some
Were hornéd like the crescent moon;
Some shed a mild and silver beam
Like Hesperus o'er the western sea;
Some dashed athwart with trains of flame,
Like worlds to death and ruin driven;
Some shone like suns, and as the chariot passed,
Eclipsed all other light.

Spirit of Nature! here!
In this interminable wilderness
Of worlds, at whose immensity
Even soaring fancy staggers,
Here is thy fitting temple.
Yet not the lightest leaf
That quivers to the passing breeze
Is less instinct with thee:
Yet not the meanest worm
That lurks in graves and fattens on the dead
Less shares thy eternal breath.
Spirit of Nature! thou!
Imperishable as this scene,
Here is thy fitting temple!

The Revolt of Islam
EXTRACT

Dedication

There is no danger to a Man, that knows
What life and death is: there's not any law
Exceeds his knowledge: neither is it lawful
That he should stoop to any other law.

Chapman

To Mary —

I

So now my summer-task is ended, Mary,
And I return to thee, mine own heart's home;
As to his Queen some victor Knight of Faëry,
Earning bright spoils for her enchanted dome;
Nor thou disdain, that ere my fame become
A star among the stars of mortal night,
If it indeed may cleave its natal gloom,
Its doubtful promise thus I would unite
With thy beloved name, thou Child of love and light.

II

The toil which stole from thee so many an hour
Is ended – and the fruit is at thy feet!
No longer where the woods to frame a bower
With interlaced branches mix and meet,
Or where with sound like many voices sweet,
Water-falls leap among wild islands green,
Which framed for my lone boat a lone retreat
Of moss-grown trees and weeds, shall I be seen:
But beside thee, where still my heart has ever been.

III

Thoughts of great deeds were mine, dear Friend, when first
The clouds which wrap this world from youth did pass
I do remember well the hour which burst
My spirit's sleep: a fresh May-dawn it was,
When I walked forth upon the glittering grass,
And wept, I knew not why: until there rose
From the near school-room, voices, that, alas!
Were but one echo from a world of woes
The harsh and grating strife of tyrants and of foes.

IV

And then I clasped my hands and looked around,
But none was near to mock my streaming eyes,
Which poured their warm drops on the sunny ground
So without shame, I spake: "I will be wise,
And just, and free, and mild, if in me lies
Such power, for I grow weary to behold
The selfish and the strong still tyrannize
Without reproach or check." I then controlled
My tears, my heart grew calm, and I was meek and bold.

V

And from that hour did I with earnest thought
Heap knowledge from forbidden mines of lore,
Yet nothing that my tyrants knew or taught
I cared to learn, but from that secret store
Wrought linked armour for my soul, before
It might walk forth to war among mankind;
Thus power and hope were strengthened more and more
Within me, till there came upon my mind
A sense of loneliness, a thirst with which I pined.

VI

Alas, that love should be a blight and snare
To those who seek all sympathies in one!
Such once I sought in vain; then black despair,
The shadow of a starless night, was thrown
Over the world in which I moved alone:
Yet never found I one not false to me,
Hard hearts, and cold, like weights of icy stone
Which crushed and withered mine, that could not be
Aught but a lifeless clog, until revived by thee.

VII

Thou Friend, whose presence on my wintry heart
Fell, like bright Spring upon some herbless plain,
How beautiful and calm and free thou wert
In thy young wisdom, when the mortal chain
Of Custom thou didst burst and rend in twain,
And walked as free as light the clouds among,
Which many an envious slave then breathed in vain
From his dim dungeon, and my spirit sprung
To meet thee from the woes which had begirt it long.

VIII

No more alone through the world's wilderness,
Although I trod the paths of high intent,
I journeyed now: no more companionless,
Where solitude is like despair, I went.
There is the wisdom of a stern content
When Poverty can blight the just and good,
When Infamy dares mock the innocent,
And cherished friends turn with the multitude
To trample: this was ours, and we unshaken stood!

IX

Now has descended a serener hour,
And with inconstant fortune, friends return;
Though suffering leaves the knowledge and the power
Which says: – Let scorn be not repaid with scorn.
And from thy side two gentle babes are born
To fill our home with smiles, and thus are we
Most fortunate beneath life's beaming morn:
And these delights, and thou, have been to me
The parents of the Song I consecrate to thee.

X

Is it, that now my inexperienced fingers
But strike the prelude of a loftier strain?
Or, must the lyre on which my spirit lingers
Soon pause in silence, ne'er to sound again,
Though it might shake the Anarch Custom's reign,
And charm the minds of men to Truth's own sway,
Holier than was Amphion's? I would fain
Reply in hope – but I am worn away,
And Death and Love are yet contending for their prey.

XI

And what art thou? I know, but dare not speak:
Time may interpret to his silent years.
Yet in the paleness of thy thoughtful cheek,
And in the light thine ample forehead wears,
And in thy sweetest smiles, and in thy tears,
And in thy gentle speech, a prophecy
Is whispered, to subdue my fondest fears:
And through thine eyes, even in thy soul I see
A lamp of vestal fire burning internally.

Prometheus Unbound
—— EXTRACT ——

Act I

Scene. A Ravine of Icy Rocks in the Indian Caucasus. Prometheus is discovered bound to the Precipice. Panthea and Ione are seated at his feet. Time, Night. During the Scene, Morning slowly breaks.

PROMETHEUS. Monarch of Gods and Dæmons, and all Spirits
But One, who throng those bright and rolling worlds
Which Thou and I alone of living things
Behold with sleepless eyes! regard this Earth
Made multitudinous with thy slaves, whom thou
Requitest for knee-worship, prayer, and praise,
And toil, and hecatombs of broken hearts,
With fear and self-contempt and barren hope.
Whilst me, who am thy foe, eyeless in hate,
Hast thou made reign and triumph, to thy scorn,
O'er mine own misery and thy vain revenge.
Three thousand years of sleep-unsheltered hours,
And moments aye divided by keen pangs
Till they seemed years, torture and solitude,
Scorn and despair – these are mine empire.
More glorious far than that which thou surveyest
From thine unenvied throne, O Mighty God!
Almighty, had I deigned to share the shame
Of thine ill tyranny, and hung not here
Nailed to this wall of eagle-baffling mountain,
Black, wintry, dead, unmeasured; without herb,
Insect, or beast, or shape or sound of life.
Ah me, alas! pain, pain ever, for ever!

No change, no pause, no hope! Yet I endure.
I ask the Earth, have not the mountains felt?
I ask yon Heaven, the all-beholding Sun,
Has it not seen? The Sea, in storm or calm,
Heaven's ever-changing Shadow, spread below,
Have its deaf waves not heard my agony?
Ah me! alas, pain, pain ever, for ever!

The crawling glaciers pierce me with the spears
Of their moon-freezing crystals; the bright chains
Eat with their burning cold into my bones.
Heaven's winged hound, polluting from thy lips
His beak in poison not his own, tears up
My heart; and shapeless sights come wandering by,
The ghastly people of the realm of dream,
Mocking me: and the Earthquake-fiends are charged
To wrench the rivets from my quivering wounds
When the rocks split and close again behind:
While from their loud abysses howling throng
The genii of the storm, urging the rage
Of whirlwind, and afflict me with keen hail.
And yet to me welcome is day and night,
Whether one breaks the hoar frost of the morn,
Or starry, dim, and slow, the other climbs
The leaden-coloured east; for then they lead
The wingless, crawling hours, one among whom
As some dark Priest hales the reluctant victim
Shall drag thee, cruel King, to kiss the blood
From these pale feet, which then might trample thee
If they disdained not such a prostrate slave.
Disdain! Ah no! I pity thee. What ruin
Will hunt thee undefended through the wide Heaven!
How will thy soul, cloven to its depth with terror,
Gape like a hell within! I speak in grief,
Not exultation, for I hate no more,

As then ere misery made me wise. The curse
Once breathed on thee I would recall. Ye Mountains,
Whose many-voiced Echoes, through the mist
Of cataracts, flung the thunder of that spell!
Ye icy Springs, stagnant with wrinkling frost,
Which vibrated to hear me, and then crept
Shuddering through India! Thou serenest Air,
Through which the Sun walks burning without beams!
And ye swift Whirlwinds, who on poised wings
Hung mute and moveless o'er yon hushed abyss,
As thunder, louder than your own, made rock
The orbed world! If then my words had power,
Though I am changed so that aught evil wish
Is dead within; although no memory be
Of what is hate, let them not lose it now!
What was that curse? for ye all heard me speak.

Lines Written on Hearing the News of the Death of Napoleon

WHAT! ALIVE and so bold, O Earth?
Art thou not over bold?
What! leapest thou forth as of old
In the light of thy morning mirth,
The last of the flock of the starry fold?
Ha! leapest thou forth as of old?
Are not the limbs still when the ghost is fled,
And canst thou move, Napoleon being dead?

How! is not thy quick heart cold?
What spark is alive on thy hearth?
How! is not his death-knell knolled?
And livest thou still, Mother Earth?
Thou wert warming thy fingers old
O'er the embers covered and cold
Of that most fiery spirit, when it fled –
What, Mother, do you laugh now he is dead?

"Who has known me of old," replied Earth,
"Or who has my story told?
It is thou who art over bold."
And the lightning of scorn laughed forth
As she sung, "To my bosom I fold
All my sons when their knell is knolled,
And so with living motion all are fed,
And the quick spring like weeds out of the dead.

"Still alive and still bold," shouted Earth,
"I grow bolder, and still more bold.
The dead fill me ten thousand fold.
Fuller of speed, and splendour, and mirth;
I was cloudy, and sullen, and cold,
Like a frozen chaos uprolled,
Till by the spirit of the mighty dead
My heart grew warm. I feed on whom I fed.

"Ay, alive and still bold," muttered Earth,
"Napoleon's fierce spirit rolled,
In terror, and blood, and gold,
A torrent of ruin to death from his birth.
Leave the millions who follow to mould
The metal before it be cold,
And weave into his shame, which like the dead
Shrouds me, the hopes that from his glory fled."

A Summer-Evening Churchyard

THE WIND has swept from the wide atmosphere
Each vapour that obscured the sunset's ray;
And pallid evening twines its beaming hair
In duskier braids around the languid eyes of day:
Silence and twilight, unbeloved of men,
Creep hand in hand from yon obscurest glen.

They breathe their spells towards the departing day,
Encompassing the earth, air, stars, and sea;
Light, sound, and motion own the potent sway,
Responding to the charm with its own mystery.
The winds are still, or the dry church-tower grass
Knows not their gentle motions as they pass.

Thou too, aërial Pile! whose pinnacles
Point from one shrine like pyramids of fire,
Obeyest in silence their sweet solemn spells,
Clothing in hues of heaven thy dim and distant spire,
Around whose lessening and invisible height
Gather among the stars the clouds of night.

The dead are sleeping in their sepulchres:
And, mouldering as they sleep, a thrilling sound,
Half sense, half thought, among the darkness stirs,
Breathed from their wormy beds all living things around,
And mingling with the still night and mute sky
Its awful hush is felt inaudibly.

Thus solemnised and softened, death is mild
And terrorless as this serenest night:
Here could I hope, like some inquiring child
Sporting on graves, that death did hide from human sight
Sweet secrets, or beside its breathless sleep
That loveliest dreams perpetual watch did keep.

To Wordsworth

POET OF Nature, thou hast wept to know
That things depart which never may return;
Childhood and youth, friendship and love's first glow,
Have fled like sweet dreams, leaving thee to mourn.
These common woes I feel. One loss is mine,
Which thou too feel'st; yet I alone deplore.
Thou wert as a lone star, whose light did shine
On some frail bark in winter's midnight roar:
Thou hast like to a rock-built refuge stood
Above the blind and battling multitude:
In honoured poverty thy voice did weave
Songs consecrate to truth and liberty,
Deserting these, thou leavest me to grieve,
Thus having been, that thou shouldst cease to be.

Hymn to Intellectual Beauty

THE AWFUL shadow of some unseen Power
Floats tho' unseen among us; visiting
This various world with as inconstant wing
As summer winds that creep from flower to flower:
Like moonbeams that behind some piny mountain shower,
It visits with inconstant glance
Each human heart and countenance;
Like hues and harmonies of evening,
Like clouds in starlight widely spread,
Like memory of music fled,
Like aught that for its grace may be
Dear and yet dearer for its mystery. –

Spirit of BEAUTY, that dost consecrate
With thine own hues all thou dost shine upon
Of human thought or form, where art thou gone?
Why dost thou pass away and leave our state,
This dim vast vale of tears, vacant and desolate?
Ask why the sunlight not for ever
Weaves rainbows o'er yon mountain river;
Why aught should fail and fade that once is shown;
Why fear and dream and death and birth
Cast on the daylight of this earth
Such gloom; why man has such a scope
For love and hate, despondency and hope;

No voice from some sublimer world hath ever
To sage or poet these responses given:
Therefore the names of Demon, Ghost, and Heaven,
Remain the records of their vain endeavour;
Frail spells, whose uttered charm might not avail to sever,
From all we hear and all we see,
Doubt, chance, and mutability.
Thy light alone, like mist o'er mountains driven,
Or music by the night wind sent
Through strings of some still instrument,
Or moonlight on a midnight stream,
Gives grace and truth to life's unquiet dream.

Love, Hope, and Self-esteem, like clouds depart
And come, for some uncertain moments lent.
Man were immortal and omnipotent,
Didst thou, unknown and awful as thou art,
Keep with thy glorious train firm state within his heart.
Thou messenger of sympathies
That wax and wane in lovers' eyes;
Thou, that to human thought art nourishment,
Like darkness to a dying flame!
Depart not as thy shadow came:
Depart not, lest the grave should be,
Like life and fear, a dark reality.

While yet a boy I sought for ghosts, and sped
Thro' many a listening chamber, cave, and ruin,
And starlight wood, with fearful steps pursuing
Hopes of high talk with the departed dead.
I called on poisonous names with which our youth is fed
I was not heard, I saw them not;
When musing deeply on the lot
Of life, at that sweet time when winds are wooing
All vital things that wake to bring
News of birds and blossoming,
Sudden, thy shadow fell on me;
I shrieked, and clasped my hands in ecstasy!

I vowed that I would dedicate my powers
To thee and thine: have I not kept the vow?
With beating heart and streaming eyes, even now
I call the phantoms of a thousand hours
Each from his voiceless grave: they have in visioned bowers
Of studious zeal or love's delight
Outwatched with me the envious night:
They know that never joy illumed my brow,
Unlinked with hope that thou wouldst free
This world from its dark slavery,
That thou, O awful LOVELINESS,
Wouldst give whate'er these words cannot express.

The day becomes more solemn and serene
When noon is past: there is a harmony
In autumn, and a lustre in its sky,
Which thro' the summer is not heard nor seen,
As if it could not be, as if it had not been!
Thus let thy power, which like the truth
Of nature on my passive youth
Descended, to my onward life supply
Its calm, to one who worships thee,
And every form containing thee,
Whom, Spirit fair thy spells did bind
To fear himself, and love all humankind.

To the Lord Chancellor

THY COUNTRY'S curse is on thee, darkest crest
Of that foul, knotted, many-headed worm
Which rends our Mother's bosom – priestly pest!
Masked resurrection of a buried form!

Thy country's curse is on thee! Justice sold,
Truth trampled, Nature's landmarks overthrown,
And heaps of fraud-accumulated gold,
Plead, loud as thunder, at Destruction's throne.

And, whilst that slow sure Angel which aye stands
Watching the beck of Mutability
Delays to execute her high commands,
And, though a nation weeps, spares thine and thee;

Oh let a father's curse be on thy soul,
And let a daughter's hope be on thy tomb,
And both on thy grey head a leaden cowl
To weigh thee down to thine approaching doom!

I curse thee by a parent's outraged love;
By hopes long cherished and too lately lost;
By gentle feelings thou couldst never prove;
By griefs which thy stern nature never crossed;

By those infantine smiles of happy light
Which were a fire within a stranger's hearth,
Quenched even when kindled, in untimely night
Hiding the promise of a lovely birth;

By those unpractised accents of young speech,
Which he who is a father thought to frame
To gentlest lore such as the wisest teach.
Thou strike the lyre of mind! Oh grief and shame!

By all the happy see in children's growth,
That undeveloped flower of budding years,
Sweetness and sadness interwoven both,
Source of the sweetest hopes and saddest fears;

By all the days, under a hireling's care,
Of dull constraint and bitter heaviness,–
Oh wretched ye if ever any were,
Sadder than orphans yet not fatherless! –

By the false cant which on their innocent lips
Must hang like poison on an opening bloom;
By the dark creeds which cover with eclipse
Their pathway from the cradle to the tomb;

By thy most impious hell, and all its terrors;
By all the grief, the madness, and the guilt
Of thine impostures, which must be their errors,
That sand on which thy crumbling power is built;

By thy complicity with lust and hate,
Thy thirst for tears, thy hunger after gold,
The ready frauds which ever on thee wait,
The servile arts in which thou hast grown old;

By thy most killing sneer, and by thy smile,
By all the acts and snares of thy black den,
And – for thou canst outweep the crocodile –
By thy false tears, those millstones braining men;

By all the hate which checks a father's love;
By all the scorn which kills a father's care;
By those most impious hands that dared remove
Nature's high bounds; by thee; and by despair; –

Yes, the despair which bids a father groan,
And cry, "My children are no longer mine;
The blood within those veins may be mine own,
But, tyrant, their polluted souls are thine!"–

I curse thee, though I hate thee not. O slave!
If thou couldst quench the earth-consuming hell
Of which thou art a demon, on thy grave
This curse should be a blessing. Fare thee well!

Sonnet: Ozymandias

I MET a traveller from an antique land
Who said: Two vast and trunkless legs of stone
Stand in the desert. Near them, on the sand,
Half sunk, a shattered visage lies, whose frown,
And wrinkled lip, and sneer of cold command.
Tell that its sculptor well those passions read
Which yet survive, stamped on these lifeless things.
The hand that mocked them and the heart that fed;
And on the pedestal these words appear:
"My name is Ozymandias, king of kings:
Look on my works, ye mighty, and despair!"
Nothing beside remains. Round the decay
Of that colossal wreck, boundless and bare,
The lone and level sands stretch far away.

The Woodman and the Nightingale

A WOODMAN whose rough heart was out of tune
(I think such hearts yet never came to good),
Hated to hear, under the stars or moon,

One nightingale in an interfluous wood
Satiate the hungry dark with melody.
And, as a vale is watered by a flood,

Or as the moonlight fills the open sky
Struggling with darkness – as a tuberose
Peoples some Indian dell with scents which lie

Like clouds above the flower from which they rose,
The singing of that happy nightingale
In this sweet forest, from the golden close

Of evening till the star of dawn may fail,
Was interfused upon the silentness,
The folded roses and the violets pale

Heard her within their slumbers; the abyss
Of heaven with all its planets; the dull ear
Of the night-cradled earth; the loneliness

Of the circumfluous waters; every sphere
And every flower and beam and cloud and wave,
And every wind of the mute atmosphere,

And every beast stretched in its rugged cave,
And every bird lulled on its mossy bough,
And every silver moth fresh from the grave,

Which is its cradle – ever from below
Aspiring like one who loves too fair, too far,
To be consumed within the purest glow

Of one serene and unapproached star,
As if it were a lamp of earthly light,
Unconscious as some human lovers are,

Itself how low, how high, beyond all height
The heaven where it would perish! – and every form
That worshipped in the temple of the night

Was awed into delight, and by the charm
Girt as with an interminable zone;
Whilst that sweet bird, whose music was a storm

Of sound, shook forth the dull oblivion
Out of their dreams; harmony became love
In every soul but one ….

———

And so this man returned with axe and saw
At evening close from killing the tall treen,
The soul of whom by nature's gentle law

Was each a wood nymph, and kept ever green
The pavement and the roof of the wild copse,
Chequering the sunlight of the blue serene

With jagged leaves, – and from the forest tops
Singing the winds to sleep – or weeping oft
Fast showers of aërial water drops

Into their mother's bosom, sweet and soft,
Nature's pure tears which have no bitterness.
Around the cradles of the birds aloft

They spread themselves into the loveliness
Of fan-like leaves, and over pallid flowers
Hang like moist clouds: or, where high branches kiss,

Make a green space among the silent bowers
Like a vast fane in a metropolis,
Surrounded by the columns and the towers

All overwrought with branch-like traceries
In which there is religion, and the mute
Persuasion of unkindled melodies,

Odours and gleams and murmurs, which the lute
Of the blind pilot-spirit of the blast
Stirs as it sails, now grave and now acute,

Wakening the leaves and waves ere it has past
To such brief unison as on the brain
One tone, which never can recur, has cast,
One accent never to return again.

Misery — A Fragment

COME, BE happy! — sit near me,
Shadow-vested Misery:
Coy, unwilling, silent bride,
Mourning in thy robe of pride,
Desolation — deified!

Come, be happy! — sit near me:
Sad as I may seem to thee,
I am happier far than thou,
Lady, whose imperial brow
Is endiademed with woe.

Misery! we have known each other,
Like a sister and a brother
Living in the same lone home,
Many years — we must live some
Hours or ages yet to come.

'Tis an evil lot, and yet
Let us make the best of it;
If love can live when pleasure dies,
We two will love, till in our eyes
This heart's Hell seem Paradise.

Come, be happy! — lie thee down
On the fresh grass newly mown,
Where the grasshopper doth sing
Merrily — one joyous thing
In a world of sorrowing!

There our tent shall be the willow,
And mine arm shall be thy pillow:
Sounds and odours, sorrowful
Because they once were sweet, shall lull
Us to slumber deep and dull.

Ha! thy frozen pulses flutter
With a love thou dar'st not utter.
Thou art murmuring – thou art weeping –
Is thine icy bosom leaping
While my burning heart lies sleeping?

Kiss me; – oh! thy lips are cold;
Round my neck thine arms enfold –
They are soft, but chill and dead;
And thy tears upon my head
Burn like points of frozen lead.

Hasten to the bridal bed –
Underneath the grave 'tis spread:
In darkness may our love be hid,
Oblivion be our coverlid –
We may rest, and none forbid.

Clasp me, till our hearts be grown
Like two shadows into one;
Till this dreadful transport may
Like a vapour fade away
In the sleep that lasts alway.

We may dream in that long sleep,
That we are not those who weep;
Even as Pleasure dreams of thee,
Life-deserting Misery,
Thou mayst dream of her with me.

Let us laugh, and make our mirth,
At the shadows of the earth,
As dogs bay the moonlight clouds,
Which, like spectres wrapt in shrouds,
Pass o'er night in multitudes.

All the wide world, beside us
Show like multitudinous
Puppets passing from a scene;
What but mockery can they mean,
Where I am – where thou hast been?

Sonnet

LIFT NOT the painted veil which those who live
Call life; though unreal shapes be pictured there,
And it but mimic all we would believe
With colours idly spread, – behind, lurk Fear
And Hope, twin Destinies; who ever weave
Their shadows, o'er the chasm, sightless and drear.
I knew one who had lifted it – he sought,
For his lost heart was tender, things to love,
But found them not, alas! nor was there aught
The world contains, the which he could approve.
Through the unheeding many he did move,
A splendour among shadows, a bright blot
Upon this gloomy scene, a Spirit that strove
For truth, and like the Preacher found it not.

Ode to the West Wind

O WILD West Wind, thou breath of Autumn's being,
Thou, from whose unseen presence the leaves dead
Are driven, like ghosts from an enchanter fleeing,

Yellow, and black, and pale, and hectic red,
Pestilence-stricken multitudes: O thou,
Who chariotest to their dark wintry bed

The winged seeds, where they lie cold and low,
Each like a corpse within its grave, until
Thine azure sister of the spring shall blow

Her clarion o'er the dreaming earth, and fill
(Driving sweet birds like flocks to feed in air)
With living hues and odours plain and hill:

Wild Spirit, which art moving everywhere;
Destroyer and preserver; hear, oh hear!

II

Thou on whose stream, 'mid the steep sky's commotion,
Loose clouds like earth's decaying leaves are shed,
Shook from the tangled boughs of Heaven and Ocean,

Angels of rain and lightning: there are spread
On the blue surface of thine airy surge,
Like the bright hair uplifted from the head

Of some fierce Mænad, even from the dim verge
Of the horizon to the zenith's height,
The locks of the approaching storm. Thou dirge

Of the dying year, to which this closing night
Will be the dome of a vast sepulchre,
Vaulted with all thy congregated might

Of vapours, from whose solid atmosphere
Black rain, and fire, and hail, will burst: Oh hear!

III

Thou who didst waken from his summer dreams
The blue Mediterranean, where he lay
Lulled by the coil of his crystalline streams,

Beside a pumice isle in Baiæ's bay,
And saw in sleep old palaces and towers
Quivering within the wave's intenser day,

All overgrown with azure moss and flowers
So sweet, the sense faints picturing them! Thou
For whose path the Atlantic's level powers

Cleave themselves into chasms, while far below
The sea-blooms and the oozy woods which wear
The sapless foliage of the ocean, know

Thy voice, and suddenly grow grey with fear,
And tremble and despoil themselves: Oh hear!

IV

If I were a dead leaf thou mightest bear;
If I were a swift cloud to fly with thee;
A wave to pant beneath thy power, and share

The impulse of thy strength, only less free
Than thou, O uncontrollable! If even
I were as in my boyhood, and could be

The comrade of thy wanderings over heaven,
As then, when to outstrip the skyey speed
Scarce seemed a vision, I would ne'er have striven

As thus with thee in prayer in my sore need.
Oh! lift me as a wave, a leaf, a cloud!
I fall upon the thorns of life! I bleed!

A heavy weight of hours has chained and bowed
One too like thee: tameless, and swift, and proud.

V

Make me thy lyre, even as the forest is:
What if my leaves are falling like its own!
The tumult of thy mighty harmonies

Will take from both a deep autumnal tone,
Sweet though in sadness. Be thou, spirit fierce
My spirit! Be thou me, impetuous one!

Drive my dead thoughts over the universe
Like withered leaves to quicken a new birth;
And, by the incantation of this verse,

Scatter, as from an unextinguished hearth
Ashes and sparks, my words among mankind!
Be through my lips to unawakened earth

The trumpet of a prophecy! O wind,
Winter comes, can Spring be far behind?

The Cloud

— EXTRACT —

I

I BRING fresh showers for the thirsting flowers,
From the seas and the streams;
I bear light shades for the leaves when laid
In their noonday dreams.
From my wings are shaken the dews that waken
The sweet buds every one,
When rocked to rest on their mother's breast,
As she dances about the sun.
I wield the flail of the lashing hail,
And whiten the green plains under,
And then again I dissolve it in rain,
And laugh as I pass in thunder.

To a Skylark
—— EXTRACT ——

I

HAIL TO thee, blithe spirit!
Bird thou never wert,
That from heaven, or near it,
Pourest thy full heart
In profuse strains of unpremeditated art.

II

Higher still and higher,
From the earth thou springest
Like a cloud of fire;
The blue deep thou wingest,
And singing still dost soar, and soaring ever singest.

III

In the golden lightning
Of the sunken sun,
O'er which clouds are brightening,
Thou dost float and run;
Like an unbodied joy whose race is just begun.

IV

The pale purple even
Melts around thy flight;
Like a star of heaven,
In the broad daylight
Thou art unseen, but yet I hear thy shrill delight.

V

Keen as are the arrows
Of that silver sphere,
Whose intense lamp narrows
In the white dawn clear,
Until we hardly see, we feel that it is there.

The Tower of Famine

AMID THE desolation of a city,
Which was the cradle, and is now the grave,
Of an extinguished people; so that pity
Weeps o'er the shipwrecks of oblivion's wave,
There stands the Tower of Famine.
It is built
Upon some prison-homes, whose dwellers rave
For bread, and gold, and blood: – pain, linked to guilt,
Agitates the light flame of their hours,
Until its vital oil is spent or spilt:
There stands the pile, a tower amid the towers
And sacred domes; each marble-ribbed roof,
The brazen-grated temples, and the bowers
Of solitary wealth! the tempest-proof
Pavilions of the dark Italian air
Are by its presence dimmed – they stand aloof,
And are withdrawn – so that the world is bare,
As if a spectre, wrapt in shapeless terror,
Amid a company of ladies fair
Should glide and glow, till it became a mirror
Of all their beauty, and their hair and hue,
The life of their sweet eyes, with all its error,
Should be absorbed, till they to marble grew.

Autumn
A DIRGE

THE WARM sun is failing, the bleak wind is wailing,
The bare boughs are sighing, the pale flowers are dying,
And the year
On the earth her deathbed, in a shroud of leaves dead,
Is lying;
Come, months, come away,
From November to May,
In your saddest array;
Follow the bier
Of the dead cold year,
And like dim shadows watch by her sepulchre.

The chill rain is falling, the nipt worm is crawling,
The rivers are swelling, the thunder is knelling
For the year;
The blithe swallows are flown, and the lizards each gone
To his dwelling;
Come, months, come away;
Put on white, black, and grey,
Let your light sisters play –
Ye, follow the bier
Of the dead cold year,
And make her grave green with tear on tear.

Ode To Liberty

Yet freedom, yet, thy banner torn but flying,
Streams like a thunder-storm against the wind. Byron.

I

A GLORIOUS people vibrated again
The lightning of the nations: Liberty,
From heart to heart, from tower to tower, o'er Spain,
Scattering contagious fire into the sky,
Gleamed. My soul spurned the chains of its dismay,
And, in the rapid plumes of song,
Clothed itself sublime and strong;
As a young eagle soars the morning clouds among,
Hovering inverse o'er its accustomed prey;
Till from its station in the heaven of fame
The Spirit's whirlwind rapt it, and the ray
Of the remotest sphere of living flame
Which paves the void, was from behind it flung,
As foam from a ship's swiftness, when there came
A voice out of the deep; I will record the same.

II

"The Sun and the serenest Moon sprang forth;
The burning stars of the abyss were hurl'd
Into the depths of heaven. The dædal earth,
That island in the ocean of the world,
Hung in its cloud of all-sustaining air:
But this divinest universe
Was yet a chaos and a curse,
For thou wert not: but power from worst producing worse,
The spirit of the beasts was kindled there,
And of the birds, and of the watery forms,
And there was war among them and despair
Within them, raging without truce or terms:
The bosom of their violated nurse
Groaned, for beasts warred on beasts, and worms on worms,
And men on men; each heart was as a hell of storms.

III

"Man, the imperial shape, then multiplied
His generations under the pavilion
Of the Sun's throne: palace and pyramid,
Temple and prison, to many a swarming million,
Were, as to mountain-wolves their ragged caves.
This human living multitude
Was savage, cunning, blind, and rude,
For thou wert not; but o'er the populous solitude,
Like one fierce cloud over a waste of waves,
Hung tyranny; beneath, sate deified
The sister-pest, congregator of slaves:
Into the shadow of her pinions wide,
Anarchs and priests who feed on gold and blood,
Till with the stain their inmost souls are dyed,
Drove the astonished herds of men from every side.

IV

" The nodding promontories, and blue isles,
And cloud-like mountains, and dividuous waves
Of Greece, basked glorious in the open smiles
Of favouring heaven: from their enchanted caves
Prophetic echoes flung dim melody
On the unapprehensive wild.
The vine, the corn, the olive mild,
Grew, savage yet, to human use unreconciled;
And like unfolded flowers beneath the sea,
Like the man's thought dark in the infant's brain,
Like aught that is which wraps what is to be,
Art's deathless dreams lay veiled by many a vein
Of Parian stone; and yet a speechless child,
Verse murmured, and Philosophy did strain
Her lidless eyes for thee; when o'er the Ægean main

V

"Athens arose: a city such as vision
Builds from the purple crags and silver towers
Of battlemented cloud, as in derision
Of kingliest masonry: the ocean floors
Pave it; the evening sky pavilions it;
Its portals are inhabited
By thunder-zoned winds, each head
Within its cloudy wings with sun-fire garlanded,
A divine work! Athens diviner yet
Gleamed with its crest of columns, on the will
Of man, as on a mount of diamond, set;
For thou wert, and thine all-creative skill
Peopled, with forms that mock the eternal dead
In marble immortality, that hill
Which was thine earliest throne and latest oracle.

VI

"Within the surface of Time's fleeting river
Its wrinkled image lies, as then it lay
Immovably unquiet, and for ever
It trembles, but it cannot pass away!
The voices of thy bards and sages thunder
With an earth-awakening blast
Through the caverns of the past;
Religion veils her eyes; Oppression shrinks aghast;
A winged sound of joy and love, and wonder,
Which soars where Expectation never flew,
Rending the veil of space and time asunder!
One ocean feeds the clouds, and streams, and dew;
One sun illumines heaven; one spirit vast
With life and love makes chaos ever new,
As Athens doth the world with thy delight renew.

VII

"Then Rome was, and from thy deep bosom fairest,
Like a wolf-club from a Cadmaean Mænad,
She drew the milk of greatness, though thy dearest
From that Elysian food was yet unweaned;
And many a deed of terrible uprightness
By thy sweet love was sanctified;
And in thy smile, and by thy side,
Saintly Camillus lived, and firm Atilius died.
But when tears stained thy robe of vestal whiteness,
And gold profaned thy Capitolian throne,
Thou didst desert, with spirit-winged lightness,
The senate of the tyrants: they sunk prone
Slaves of one tyrant. Palatinus sighed
Faint echoes of Ionian song; that tone
Thou didst delay to hear, lamenting to disown.

VIII

"From what Hyrcanian glen or frozen hill,
Or piny promontory of the Arctic main,
Or utmost islet inaccessible,
Didst thou lament the ruin of thy reign,
Teaching the woods and waves, and desert rocks,
And every Naiad's ice-cold urn,
To talk in echoes sad and stern,
Of that sublimest lore which man had dared unlearn
For neither didst thou watch the wizard flocks
Of the Scald's dreams, nor haunt the Druid's sleep.
What if the tears rained through thy shattered locks,
Were quickly dried? for thou didst groan, not weep,
When from its sea of death to kill and burn,
The Galilean serpent forth did creep,
And made thy world an undistinguishable heap.

IX

"A thousand years the Earth cried 'Where art thou?'
And then the shadow of thy coming fell
On Saxon Alfred's olive-cinctured brow:
And many a warrior-peopled citadel,
Like rocks, which fire lifts out of the flat deep,
Arose in sacred Italy,
Frowning o'er the tempestuous sea
Of kings, and priests, and slaves, in tower-crowned majesty:
That multitudinous anarchy did sweep,
And burst around their walls like idle foam,
Whilst from the human spirit's deepest deep,
Strange melody with love and awe struck dumb
Dissonant arms; and Art which cannot die,
With divine want traced on our earthly home
Fit imagery to pave heaven's everlasting dome."

Adonaïs

AN ELEGY ON THE DEATH OF JOHN KEATS
—————— EXTRACT ——————

I

I WEEP for Adonaïs – he is dead!
Oh, weep for Adonaïs! though our tears
Thaw not the frost which binds so dear a head!
And thou, sad Hour, selected from all years
To mourn our loss, rouse thy obscure compeers,
And teach them thine own sorrow.
Say: "With me
Died Adonaïs, till the Future dares
Forget the Past, his fate and fame shall be
An echo and a light unto eternity!

II

Where wert thou, mighty Mother, when he lay,
When thy son lay, pierced by the shaft which flies
In darkness? where was lorn Urania
When Adonaïs died? With veiled eyes,
'Mid listening Echoes, in her Paradise
She sate, while one, with soft enamoured breath,
Rekindled all the fading melodies,
With which, like flowers that mock the corse beneath,
He had adorned and hid the coming bulk of Death.

III

Oh, weep for Adonaïs – he is dead!
Wake, melancholy Mother, wake and weep!
Yet wherefore? Quench within their burning bed
Thy fiery tears, and let thy loud heart keep,
Like his, a mute and uncomplaining sleep;
For he is gone, where all things wise and fair
Descend: – Oh, dream not that the amorous Deep
Will yet restore him to the vital air;
Death feeds on his mute voice, and laughs at our despair.

IV

Most musical of mourners, weep again!
Lament anew, Urania! – He died,
Who was the Sire of an immortal strain.
Blind, old, and lonely, when his country's pride
The priest, the slave, and the liberticide,
Trampled and mocked with many a loathed rite
Of lust and blood; he went, unterrified,
Into the gulf of death; but his clear Sprite
Yet reigns o'er earth; the third among the sons of light.

V

Most musical of mourners, weep anew!
Not all to that bright station dared to climb:
And happier they their happiness who knew,
Whose tapers yet burn through that night of time
In which suns perished; others more sublime,
Struck by the envious wrath of man or God,
Have sunk, extinct in their refulgent prime;
And some yet live, treading the thorny road,
Which leads, through toil and hate, to Fame's serene abode.

VI

But now, thy youngest, dearest one, has perished,
The nursling of thy widowhood, who grew,
Like a pale flower by some sad maiden cherished,
And fed with true love tears instead of dew;
Most musical of mourners, weep anew!
Thy extreme hope, the loveliest and the last,
The bloom, whose petals nipt before they blew
Died on the promise of the fruit, is waste;
The broken lily lies – the storm is overpast.

VII

To that high Capital, where kingly Death
Keeps his pale court in beauty and decay,
He came; and bought, with price of purest breath,
A grave among the eternal. – Come away!
Haste, while the vault of blue Italian day
Is yet his fitting charnel-roof! while still
He lies, as if in dewy sleep he lay;
Awake him not! Surely he takes his fill
Of deep and liquid rest, forgetful of all ill.

VIII

He will awake no more, Oh, never more!
Within the twilight chamber spreads apace
The shadow of white Death, and at the door
Invisible Corruption waits to trace
His extreme way to her dim dwelling-place;
The eternal Hunger sits, but pity and awe
Soothe her pale rage, nor dares she to deface
So fair a prey, till darkness and the law
Of change, shall o'er his sleep the mortal curtain draw.

The Dirge

OLD WINTER was gone
In his weakness back to the mountains hoar,
And the spring came down
From the planet that hovers upon the shore
Where the sea of sunlight encroaches
On the limits of wintry night;
If the land, and the air, and the sea,
Rejoice not when spring approaches,
We did not rejoice in thee,
Ginevra!

She is still, she is cold
On the bridal couch,
One step to the white deathbed,
And one to the charnel – and one, Oh where?
The dark arrow fled
In the noon.

Ere the sun through heaven once more has rolled
The rats in her heart
Will have made their nest,
And the worms be alive in her golden hair;
While the spirit that guides the sun
Sits throned in his flaming chair,
She shall sleep.

Epipsychidion

Verses addressed to the noble and unfortunate Lady Emilia Viviani

Now Imprisoned in the Convent of St. Anne, Pisa

——————— EXTRACT ———————

SWEET SPIRIT! Sister of that orphan one,
Whose empire is the name thou weepest on
In my heart's temple I suspend to thee
These votive wreaths of withered memory.

Poor captive bird! who, from they narrow cage,
Pourest such music, that it might assuage
The rugged hearts of those who prisoned thee,
Were they not deaf to all sweet melody;
This song shall be thy rose: its petals pale
Are dead, indeed, my adored Nightingale!
But soft and fragrant is the faded blossom,
And it has no thorn left to wound thy bosom.

High, spirit-singed Heart! who dost for ever
Beat thine unfeeling bars with vain endeavour,
Till those bright plumes of thought, in which arrayed
It over-soared this low and worldly shade,
Lie shattered; and thy panting wounded breast
Stains with dear blood its unmaternal nest!
I weep vain tears: blood would less bitter be,
Yet poured forth gladlier, could it profit thee.

Lines
IF I WALK IN AUTUMN'S EVEN

IF I walk in Autumn's even
While the dead leaves pass.
If I look on Spring's soft heaven,
Something is not there which was.
Winter's wondrous frost and snow,
Summer's clouds, where are they now?

To Jane

THE KEEN stars were twinkling,
And the fair moon was rising among them,
Dear Jane!
The guitar was tinkling,
But the notes were not sweet till you sung them
Again.
As the moon's soft splendour
O'er the faint cold starlight of heaven
Is thrown,
So your voice most tender
To the strings without soul had them given
Its own.

The stars will awaken,
Though the moon sleep a full hour later,
To-night;
No leaf will be shaken
Whilst the dews of your melody scatter
Delight.
Though the sound overpowers,
Sing again, with your dear voice revealing
A tone
Of some world far from ours,
Where music and moonlight and feeling
Are one.

Lines
WHEN THE LAMP IS SHATTERED

WHEN THE lamp is shattered,
The light in the dust lies dead –
When the cloud is scattered,
The rainbow's glory is shed.
When the lute is broken,
Sweet tones are rememberd not;
When the lips have spoken,
Loved accents are soon forgot.

As music and splendour
Survive not the lamp and the lute,
The heart's echoes render
No song when the spirit is mute: –
No song but sad dirges,
Like the wind through a ruined cell,
Or the mournful surges
That ring the dead seaman's knell.

When the hearts have once mingled,
Love first leaves the well-built nest;
The weak one is singled
To endure what it once possessed.
O, Love! who bewailest
The frailty of all things here,
Why choose you the frailest
For your cradle, your home, and your bier?

Its passions will rock thee,
As the storms rock the ravens on high
Bright reason will mock thee,
Like the sun from a wintry sky,
From thy nest every rafter
Will rot, and thine eagle home
Leave thee naked to laughter,
When leaves fall and cold winds come.

Sonnets From the Greek of Moschus

EXTRACT

II

PAN LOVED his neighbour Echo, but that child
Of Earth and Air pined for the Satyr leaping.
The Satyr loved with wasting madness wild
The bright nymph Lyda – and so the three went weeping.
As Pan loved Echo, Echo loved the Satyr;
The Satyr, Lyda, and thus love consumed them.
And thus to each – which was a woeful matter
To bear what they inflicted, justice doomed them;
For in as much as each might hate the lover,
Each, loving, so was hated. – Ye that love not
Be warned; in thought turn this example over,
That, when ye love, the like return ye prove not.

England in 1819

AN OLD, mad, blind, despised, and dying king, –
Princes, the dregs of their dull race, who flow
Through public scorn – mud from a muddy spring,
Rulers, who neither see, nor feel, nor know,
But leech-like to their fainting country cling,
Till they drop, blind in blood, without a blow, –
A people starved and stabbed in the untilled field,
An army, which liberticide and prey
Makes as a two-edged sword to all who wield,
Golden and sanguine laws which tempt and slay,
Religion Christless, Godless – a book sealed;
A Senate – Time's worst statute unrepealed, –
Are graves, from which a glorious Phantom may
Burst, to illumine our tempestuous day.

Time

UNFATHOMABLE SEA! whose waves are years,
Ocean of Time, whose waters of deep woe
Are brackish with the salt of human tears!
Thou shoreless flood, which in thy ebb and flow
Claspest the limits of mortality!
And sick of prey, yet howling on for more,
Vomitest thy wrecks on its inhospitable shore;
Treacherous in calm, and terrible in storm,
Who shall put forth on thee,
Unfathomable Sea?

Index to First Lines

Notes on Illustrations